Like a Fish in Water

Yoga for Children

Like a Fish in Water

Yoga for Children

Text and Illustrations by

Isabelle Koch

Inner Traditions
Rochester, Vermont

Inner Traditions International
One Park Street
Rochester, Vermont 05767
www.InnerTraditions.com

First U.S. edition published by Inner Traditions in 1999

First published in New Zealand by RSVP Publishing Company Limited in 1998

Library of Congress Cataloging-in-Publication Data

Koch, Isabelle.
Like a fish in water : yoga for children / text and illustrations by Isabelle Koch. — 1st U.S. ed.
p.   cm.
ISBN 0-89281-773-9 (alk. paper)
1. Yoga, Hatha, for children.   2. Exercise for children.   I. Title.
RA781.7.K63   1999
613.7'046'083—dc21   99-28576
CIP

Printed and bound in Hong Kong

10 9 8 7 6 5 4 3 2 1

This book was typeset in Adobe Garamond

Preface

The practice of Yoga provides mental peace and, at the same time, a consciousness of one's own body. Certain postures develop suppleness and balance, others strengthen muscles.

I started to practice Yoga at the age of fifty and I haven't stopped since. For several years I took Sri Mahesh's classes in Paris and the seminars that he organized in Provence, happy at the communion which united all the participants. Now I practice by myself every morning as a start to my day.

Yoga is so much a part of my life now that in my books, Babar's daughter practices it with two friends. This little girl is called Isabelle, in honor of Isabelle Koch—whom I presented to Mahesh.

Since that time Isabelle has become a Yoga teacher and the mother of a little girl called Garance. And she has realized what I only imagined: to teach Yoga to her daughter. I never thought that children could really practice Yoga. Of course they are supple, but can they accept the slow rhythm which follows the breathing (as they never rest—well, only in their sleep!)? As a Yoga teacher, Isabelle Koch has found how to speak to them and how to interest them.

Laurent de Brunhoff
creator of Babar the elephant

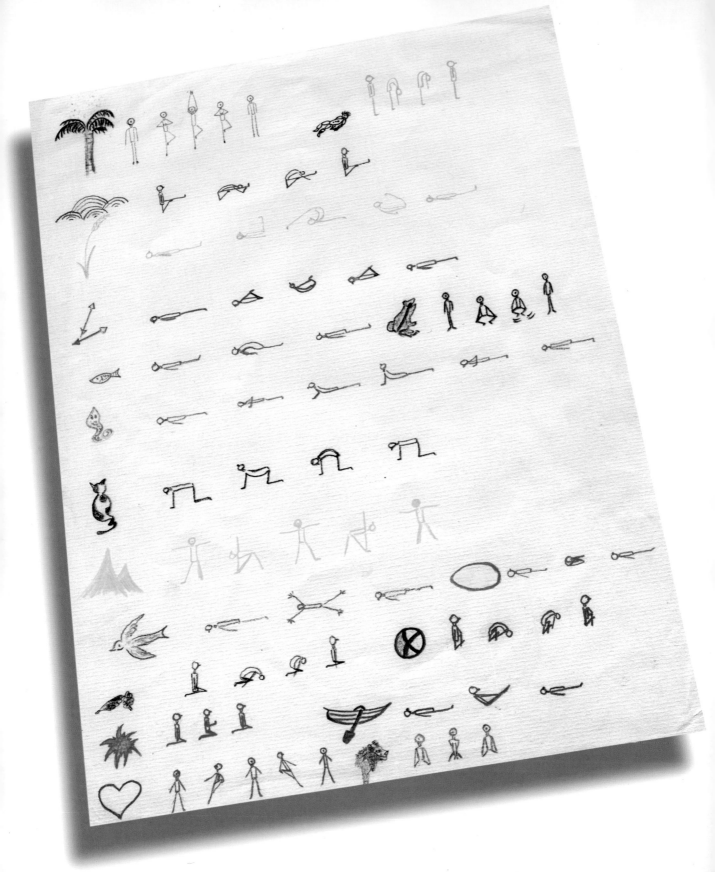

Contents

Hello.
The little girl that you see
in this picture, Garance,
and Isabelle, her mother,
have produced this book
to share their joy of Yoga with you.

It is a story about your body, your breathing
and the images that you will invent in your mind.
Postures are placed in an order that is good to follow.
And when you get to know them well,
you will be able to do them easily and without tension.
As you discover the Yoga postures,
you will feel that they are good for you and help you to grow up.

It's best to do the postures together with special Yogic breathing.
When you breathe in through the nose,
inhalation starts in the tummy and continues in the chest,
which opens itself and rises toward the throat.
When you breathe out through the mouth, the process reverses;
the chest comes down, closes itself, and the belly slightly hollows.
Imagine that you are inhaling further up than the top of your head,
and that you exhale further down than the tips of your toes.

You will do Yoga as you feel it.
Your Mummy and Daddy can help and can enjoy the practice with you.
If you do not know how to read yet,
ask them to explain what is happening in each picture.
It's up to you to play now!

The Legend

Once upon a time long ago, an enchanted fish listened attentively to the god Shiva as he taught the secrets of Yoga to his wife, the goddess Parvati. The fish, who by stealth had learned this high science, was seen by the god Shiva and was driven away. The fish swam for a long time and finally ran aground on a river shore in India. Here it transformed itself, by the miracle of Yoga, into a human being. Welcomed by the Indian people, the fish was named Matsyendra— Lord of the Fish. And in thanks for their hospitality, Matsyendra taught them the Yoga postures.

The Mudras

The Mudras—the signs—
were formerly used as a language by the Indian pilgrims who took months,
sometimes even years, to reach holy places by foot. During their journey
they often met people who spoke languages that they did not understand.
At each stage, they used gestures to communicate with wise men who welcomed
them into their hermitages. These gestures became the language of the Mudras,
which were adopted by the Yogis for meditation. Meditation is simply deep
thought on the meaning of life.

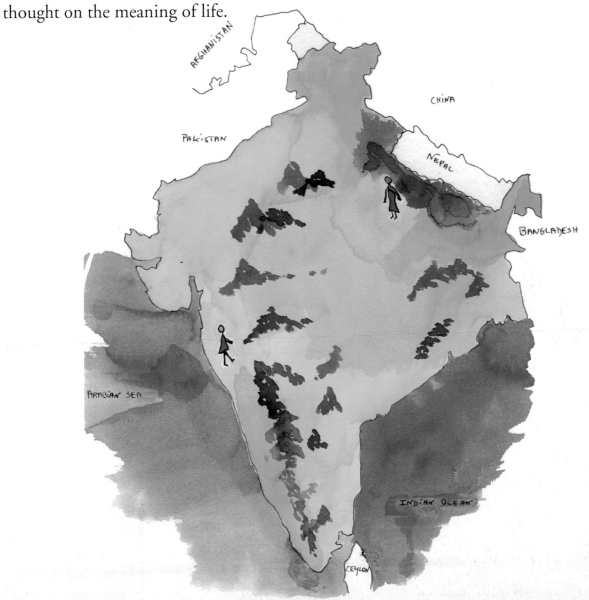

The Rag Doll

Standing up, legs together, arms by the side, I breathe without effort. Slowly, really slowly, I let my head fall, then my shoulders, my arms, my torso, keeping my legs straight. I stay like this for several moments, head falling toward the ground. It is good for the blood circulation in my head. I come up slowly, softly, vertebra after vertebra, raising my head last. I stay up, still and silent.
I feel good between the sky and the earth.

The Palm Tree

I am a tree, tall and strong.
My straight leg is the trunk,
my bent leg is a twisted branch.
My arms are the top of the tree,
which grows toward the Sun.
Standing feet together,
I bring my right foot up to my groin.
My hands are joined in front of my chest.
I inhale deeply
and lift my arms higher than my head.
Thumbs together and fingers apart,
I stay several moments without moving at all.
Then I release my arms, then my bent leg.
I repeat on the other side.
The palm tree is a really good posture for concentration and balance.

The Triangle

Legs and arms apart,
I open my left foot while inhaling.
Then I exhale,
putting my left hand on my left foot,
and I look at my right hand stretched
over my head to show me the light.
I come up slowly, breathing in,
and I repeat on the other side.
It is good fun stretching the small of your back,
the arms and legs.
The triangle shapes the legs, strengthens the ankles,
improves the arches of the feet
and builds up the chest.

The Frog

I am a frog croaking on the bank of a pond. Standing up, heels together,
on tiptoe, open, I inhale, my back straight, my arms along my body.
While exhaling, I go down crouching on my heels, knees apart. Hands on
my knees, I maintain a really straight back and I jump like a frog,
before maintaining the balance on my tiptoe during several breaths.
The frog works the balance, and strengthens the back, knees, and ankles.

The Lion

I am a big, majestic lion roaring with a beautiful, strong voice.
Sitting on my opened knees, I place my hands
between them, fingers backward.
Then I lean forward, arms straight.
Raising my head, I open my mouth and stick out my tongue as far as it will go.
I open my eyes as wide as I can and concentrate on the space between my
eyebrows. I inhale through the nose, and while exhaling slowly
I make a regular sound from my throat.

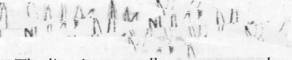

The lion is an excellent posture to do when we have a sore throat
or earache or a blocked nose.
And it gives you a beautiful voice.

Yoga Mudra

I sit, my back straight, legs crossed and my hands opened on my knees,
forefingers bent under thumbs.
I inhale deeply.
I exhale and bring my forehead toward the floor.
When I need to breathe in I slowly lift my body and unfold my spine (which is
made up of tiny bones fitting one over the other in the shape of a snake),
raising my head last.
After doing this movement three times in a row,
my back is straight and I feel relaxed.

Yoga Mudra is a gesture of the entire body
that we keep for a moment before release.
When we bow and the forehead goes toward the floor,
it shows an attitude of thanks toward life.

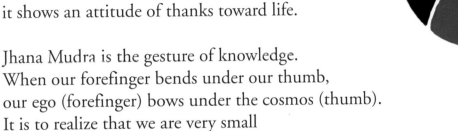

Jhana Mudra is the gesture of knowledge.
When our forefinger bends under our thumb,
our ego (forefinger) bows under the cosmos (thumb).
It is to realize that we are very small
when compared to the universe.

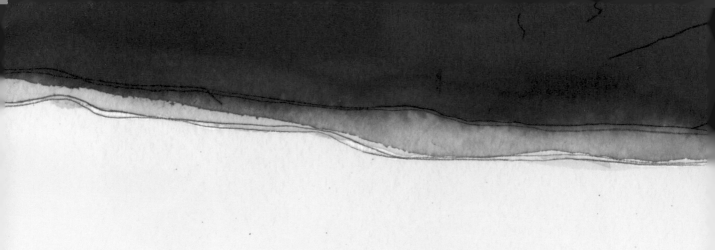

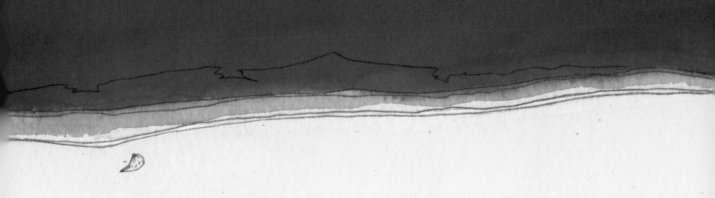

Maha Mudra

I sit on the bones of my bottom,
my left leg stretched in front of me and my right leg bent,
my right foot against my groin.
My back straight, I inhale, raise my chest and lower my chin.
Then I exhale as I bend over my left leg, catching my ankle and my calf.
I stay several moments, head toward the knee, elbows open.
While inhaling I softly straighten my back,
imagining that I am a sprouting flower.
My tail bone is the root, my back is the stem,
and my head and neck are the petal and the pistil.
I change sides.
I feel that my head and body are calmer.

Maha Mudra:
Maha means big. Maha Mudra means the big posture of the entire body.

The Autumn Leaf

I am an autumn leaf.
I sit on my knees, back straight, arms down.
I inhale deeply and exhale while slowly bending forward.
My forehead touches the floor like an autumn leaf touches the earth.
I hold the posture over several breaths.

I feel that I am breathing through my back and my ribs.
Inhaling, my back raises itself, my rib cage stretches.
Exhaling, my back sinks, my ribs tighten.
I come up really slowly.
I feel a sensation of well-being.

Shiva Mudra

Sitting on my heels, I open my arms a bit wider than my body,
palms of my hands facing each other.
As slowly as possible I join my hands in front of my chest
and press them gently together.
I breathe calmly.
I close my eyes to observe the sensations in my hands
(which are the most sensitive part of the body).

Shiva Mudra:
Shiva, God of the Yogi, is sometimes represented as half-man, half-woman.
Shiva Mudra is the gesture which joins the masculine and feminine energy
which is in all of us.
In India people say hello to each other in this way.

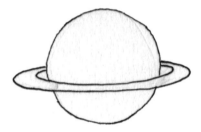

The Fetus

Lying on my back, elbows open and fingers crossed behind my head,
(or hands on my knees),
I breathe in deeply.
I bend my legs and press my knees against my chest,
my thighs pushing on my belly.
I exhale, bringing my forehead to my knees.
I bring my head back to the floor and breathe naturally.
I do it again, slowly, three times.
Then I bring my knees to the floor on my left side, head turned to the opposite
side. I stay for several seconds, then I change sides.
The fetus recalls the position we had in our mother's belly. It is a really good
tummy and back massage, an agreeable posture which can unblock your spine.

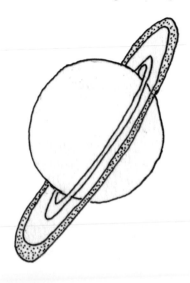

The Boat

I am a strong boat which can travel
over the ocean in all weather.
Lying on my back,
I put my hands on my thighs.
I inhale, then exhale deeply in my tummy
while I raise my head,
my shoulders and my legs.

I keep the small of my back on the floor.
Feet and head are on the same level.
I stay several moments in this position,
feeling the strength of my tummy muscles.
Then I relax completely on the floor.

The boat strengthens the stomach muscles and the back.

The Plough

I am a plough in the earth. I lie on my back, arms along my body and palms on the floor. I exhale, engage my stomach muscles and pull my legs over my head, touching the tip of my toes on the floor. I keep the posture for several moments while breathing through the small of my back. My legs and feet are the plough-share which traces a furrow in the soil. Then I exhale, bringing my spine slowly back to the floor, then my legs and head, as if I would leave in the earth a trace of the impressions of each vertebra, one after the other, the tail bone last.

The Fish

I dream that I swim like a fish.
On my back, arms by my side, I arch my back and lift myself off the ground,
resting the top half of my body on my elbows.
I let my head drop so the crown is resting on the ground.
I breathe deeply with my mouth open like a fish,
and I let the yawning come freely.
Breathing deeply in this position, I come down, again using my elbows.
Released, I feel my tummy and chest open.

The Stretching Cat

I am a cat which adores stretching itself in all directions.
My spine is supple, very supple!
On all fours, hands and knees slightly apart,
I inhale, lift my head and curve my back.
Keeping my arms and legs still,
I breathe out and drop my head,
arching my back into the air.
I do this posture several times, really slowly to feel my back.
The stretching cat will gently exercise your neck, shoulders, and entire spine.

The Bow

I am the bow which shoots arrows. My arms are stretched like the bowstring.
On my tummy I bend and open my knees, grasping my ankles.
I inhale deeply, pull on my feet and raise my chest.
I keep my tummy on the ground and my arms stretched.
I concentrate on the opening of my chest.
When I need to exhale, I slowly release this position.
The bow is a good massage for the tummy's interior muscles.
It makes the spine elastic and expands the chest and lungs.

The Cobra

I am a cobra and I am sliding along on the desert sand.
The cobra is a snake capable of lifting up its body to face danger.
Lying on my tummy—forehead pressed against the floor,
feet together, hands alongside my chest—
I inhale deeply, then I lift up my head and my chest
while pushing backward on my arms, shoulders, and head.
When I need to exhale,
I slowly bring chest and head to the floor,
elbows bent against my body.

The cobra strengthens the middle of your back,
helps to remove stiffness in the neck and spine,
and stimulates appetite.

The Flying Bird

I fly! I lie on my tummy, forehead on the floor,
legs and arms wide apart.
I inhale deeply while I slowly lift my head,
then my arms and legs which become my wings.
I open my fingers and toes as far apart as possible.
I keep the posture holding my breath. I feel so light,
like a bird. When I need to breathe out, I release slowly.

The flying bird helps to stretch the body
to its maximum, and tones the muscles
to become smooth and slender.

The Zig-Zag

Resting gently on my back,
I put my left foot on my right knee
and my right hand on my left knee.
While exhaling, I use my right hand to gently bring
my left knee to the floor,
and turn my head to the opposite side.
For several moments I breathe calmly in the zig-zag.
Then I slowly bring my back to the floor, legs and arms totally relaxed.

46

Then I make the zig-zag on the other side.
And once again on each side.
The zig-zag is an excellent posture for unlocking your back.

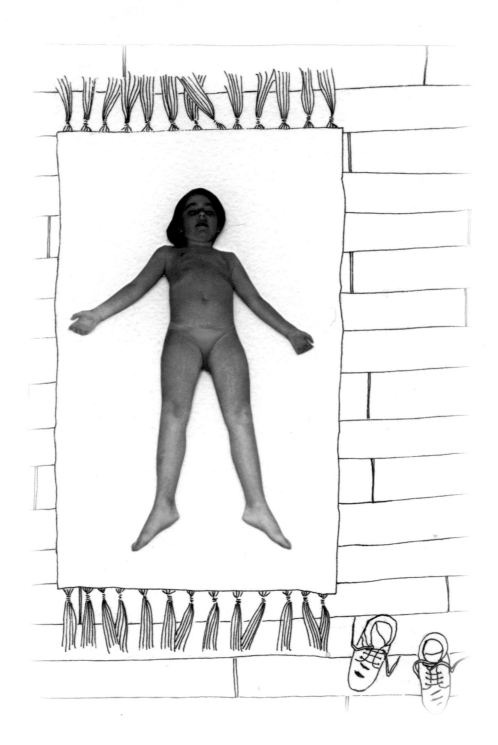

The Lying Rag Doll

I lie on my back, arms along my body, palms turned up toward the sky.
I open my feet slightly to feel as comfortable as possible.
I release my body completely and it feels like I am sinking
into a bed of cotton.
I let my breathing become natural, without effort.
I concentrate on my breathing; I do not think of anything else.
Then I adopt a square, rhythmic breathing pattern like this:

1. I inhale (take in air).
2. I hold my breath.
3. I exhale (I blow out the air).
4. I hold my breath.
I do this exercise 10 times. Then I resume my natural breathing pattern.

The lying rag doll relaxes the nerves and the brain, removes fatigue,
teaches concentration, and calms the emotions.

Anuloma Viloma

I sit comfortably. I put my middle finger (the biggest) and forefinger (the one which points out the piece of cake I want!) in the middle of my forehead.
Then—now with the thumb, now with the ring finger—I block one nostril after the other, taking care to breathe air out and breathe air in from the same nostril.
I breathe in this way regularly and slowly, without pressing too hard on the side of the nose where a little hollow is formed.
It is time to feel if I can breathe as well from the right nostril as from the left nostril, and to blow my nose.
I breathe deeply from both nostrils, as if I am smelling a flower's perfume.

Breathing and Relaxation Exercises

Here are several breathing and relaxation exercises
that I repeat several times in a row, still lying on my back.

I inhale deeply: the act of breathing in starts in the tummy
(which slightly swells) and continues in the chest,
which opens itself and rises toward the throat.
For exhaling, the process reverses: my chest comes down,
closes itself, and my belly slightly hollows.
I imagine that I inhale further up than the top of my head,
and exhale further down than the tips of my toes.

A Yoga breath is to feel the gentle fullness in every moment.
It is almost like making time stand still.
Imagine watching a beautiful eagle flying on the distant horizon.
Perhaps it is going from east to west.
Imagine you are the eagle with powerful wings and beautiful soft feathers,
flying in a spiral, higher and higher above a mountain.
Your body is the mountain.
Your awareness is the spiral.
Your breath is the eagle.

The Balloon
Inhale: I swell like a balloon.
Stop: I feel inflated and big.
Exhale: I collapse and gather myself.
Stop: I am centered.

The Flower
My hands are open toward the sky like a flower's petals.
For a moment I play being a flower. I open my hands extremely slowly
and I feel the warmth of the sun in the hollow of my palms.
I imagine that the light falls like golden snow.
Then I slowly close my hands.

Sounds
I listen to some faraway sounds, then to the closest sounds.
I imagine that I tune inside my ears to listen to the sounds of my body.
Or again, I listen to a sound for its full duration,
keeping it in my head as long as possible.

The Magic Word
I choose a word which makes me feel good.
For example: softness, dream, wind, sunshine, love. . . .
And I repeat it in my head on each exhalation (breathing out).

Yawning
When I feel tired, I yawn.
To yawn about ten times is as good as taking a short nap.

The word Yoga means to join or unite.
It is the means by which our mind can be made still,
quiet and free from all distractions.

The body is the house in which heart and mind are reunited.
When we practice Yoga,
we try to bring back together
the light of our heart and the light of our mind
to make them one—a natural process
like the light of the night replacing the light of the day.

The author would like to thank Yannick Noah and Laurent de Brunhoff
for their interest in the project, and Sri Mahesh for his teachings.